A TRIP TO THE POLICE STATION

DE VISITA EN LA ESTACIÓN DE POLICÍA

Josie Keogh

Traducción al español: Eduardo Alamán

PowerKiDS
press™

New York

Published in 2013 by The Rosen Publishing Group, Inc.
29 East 21st Street, New York, NY 10010

First Edition

Editor: Amelie von Zumbusch
Book Design: Ashley Drago

Traducción al español: Eduardo Alamán

Photo Credits: Cover © UpperCut Images/age fotostock; pp. 5, 17, 18, 22 Shutterstock.com; p. 6 Darrin Klimek/Digital Vision/Thinkstock; pp. 9, 10 Jupiterimages/Photos.com/Thinkstock; p. 13 Darrin Klimek/Digital Vision/Getty Images; p. 14 © www.iStockphoto.com/Darren Mower; p. 21 UpperCut Images/Getty Images; p. 24 (middle) iStockphoto/Thinkstock.

Library of Congress Cataloging-in-Publication Data

Keogh, Josie.
[A trip to the police station. English and Spanish]
 A trip to the police station = De visita en la estación de policía / by Josie Keogh; [translated by Eduardo Alamán]. — 1st ed.
    p. cm. — (Powerkids readers: my community = Mi comunidad)
 Includes index.
 ISBN 978-1-4488-7829-1 (library binding)
 1. Police—Juvenile literature. I. Title. II. Title: Visita en la estación de policía.
 HV7922.K484 2013
 363.2—dc23
                                2011052879

Websites: Due to the changing nature of Internet links, PowerKids Press has developed an online list of websites related to the subject of this book. This site is updated regularly. Please use this link to access the list:
www.powerkidslinks.com/pkrc/police/

Manufactured in the United States of America

CPSIA Compliance Information: Batch #CS12PK: For Further Information contact Rosen Publishing, New York, New York at 1-800-237-9932

CONTENTS

CONTENIDO

We went to the police station.

Fuimos a la estación
de policía.

Pat's dad is the chief.

El papá de Pat es el jefe.

7

We met a police dog.

_____

Conocimos un perro policía.

9

10

His name was Max.

Su nombre es Max.

11

We saw Officer May's badge.

Vimos la insignia de la oficial May.

14

Joe tried on her hat.

Joe se puso su gorra.

15

We saw Officer Reed's car.

Vimos la patrulla del oficial Reed.

18

Then he had to go.

Luego, el oficial se fue
a trabajar.

19

A man stole a car.

Un hombre robó un auto.

21

The police caught the man!

———————————————————

¡La policía lo atrapó!

23

WORDS TO KNOW / PALABRAS QUE DEBES SABER

arrest: To hold someone by law.

arresto: Detener a una persona.

criminal: A person who breaks the law.

delincuente: Una persona que quiebra la ley.

uniform: Clothes worn by a group of people.

uniforme: La ropa que usa un grupo de personas.